Greenhouse Gardening For Kids

A Practical Guide For Children To
Plant And Harvest Fruits, Vegetables,
Flowers And Herbs All-Year Round
(With Farm Produce Recipes)

Helen A. Krick

Copyright © 2024
Helen A. Krick

All rights reserved. No part of this publication may be reproduced, distributed, or transmitted in any form or by any means, including photocopying, recording, or other electronic or mechanical methods, without the prior written permission of the publisher, except in the case of brief quotations embodied in critical reviews and certain other noncommercial uses permitted by copyright law.

Introduction.. 6
Chapter 1: What is greenhouse gardening and why is it fun and educational for kids............... 10
    Safety guidelines for kids' greenhouse gardening.. 16
Chapter 2: Getting Started with Greenhouse Gardening :Choosing the right greenhouse for kids.. 22
    Setting up a greenhouse space...................... 28
    Essential tools and supplies for kids' greenhouse gardening................................. 35
Chapter 3: Selecting Plants for the Greenhouse :Easy-to-grow plants for kids.......................... 42
    Vegetables, herbs, flowers, and fruits suitable for greenhouse gardening............................... 49
    Planning and designing a kid-friendly greenhouse garden.. 55
Chapter 4: Greenhouse Gardening Practical Activities.. 62
    Hands-on experiments and projects............... 62
    Learning about ecosystems, pollination, and beneficial insects through practicals............... 74
    Keeping a garden journal and recording observations.. 80
Chapter 5: Fun Activities and Games for Greenhouse Gardening.. 87
    Garden-themed crafts and DIY projects........... 89
    Nature-inspired games and activities for kids. 94
    Hosting a greenhouse gardening party for friends and family.. 100
Chapter 6: Planting and Propagating............. 107

Starting seeds indoors............................111
Transplanting seedlings into the greenhouse..... 117
Propagating plants from cuttings and divisions... 123

Chapter 7: Caring for Plants in the Greenhouse.. 130

Watering and fertilizing tips for kids.............. 130
Pest and disease management................... 135
Pruning, staking, and training plants for healthy growth.. 140

Chapter 8: Harvesting and Enjoying the Fruits of Your Labor...145

Knowing when to harvest............................ 145
Harvesting techniques for kids..................... 149

Conclusion... 154

Bonus: Recipes and crafts using greenhouse-grown produce and flowers....... 156

Introduction

Imagine a place where the air is thick with the scent of herbs, where vibrant flowers bloom year-round, and where the humble seed transforms into a bounty of delicious fruits and vegetables. Welcome to the magical world of greenhouse gardening, where children can cultivate their curiosity, creativity, and connection with nature.

In "Greenhouse Gardening for Kids," we invite young gardeners on an exciting journey into the heart of the greenhouse—a sanctuary brimming with life and possibilities. From planting seeds to harvesting the fruits of their labor, this book is a comprehensive guide that empowers children to become stewards of the earth while discovering the joy and wonder of growing their own food and flowers.

But greenhouse gardening is more than just a hobby—it's a gateway to a lifetime of learning and exploration. As kids dig their hands into the soil and watch seeds sprout into seedlings, they develop invaluable skills in patience, responsibility, and problem-solving. They learn about the natural cycles of growth and decay, the importance of water and sunlight, and the delicate balance of ecosystems.

Moreover, greenhouse gardening is a multi-sensory experience that engages all five senses, allowing children to fully immerse themselves in the wonders of the natural world. They can feel the texture of leaves, smell the fragrance of flowers, taste the sweetness of ripe tomatoes, hear the buzz of pollinators, and see the kaleidoscope of colors that paint the garden landscape.

But perhaps the greatest gift of greenhouse gardening is the sense of connection it fosters—not only to the plants themselves but also to the planet we call home. As children witness the miracles of growth and transformation firsthand, they develop a profound appreciation for the Earth's abundance and beauty. They learn to respect and care for the environment, knowing that their actions have the power to nurture and sustain life. Kids also get to bond with parents as they go through every activity and practicals with guidelines from a parent or guardian. This is a great way to have a good connection with your kids!

So, whether you're a parent or guardian, "Greenhouse Gardening for Kids" invites you to embark on a journey of discovery and delight with your lovely kids. Together, let's sow the seeds of curiosity, cultivate the soil of creativity, and harvest the fruits of connection. For in the greenhouse garden, every moment is an opportunity to grow, learn, and thrive. Welcome to the adventure of a lifetime!

Chapter 1: What is greenhouse gardening and why is it fun and educational for kids

Greenhouse gardening offers a captivating and enriching experience for children, blending fun and education in a vibrant setting. It involves cultivating plants within a controlled environment, typically a structure made of transparent materials like glass or plastic, allowing sunlight to penetrate while trapping heat to create a warm, nurturing atmosphere for plant growth.

Here's a detailed exploration of why greenhouse gardening is both enjoyable and educational for kids:

1. Hands-on Learning:

Greenhouse gardening provides a hands-on approach to learning about plants, from seed germination to harvest. Children actively engage in every step of the process, fostering a deeper understanding of plant life cycles, growth patterns, and the importance of caring for living organisms.

2. Scientific Exploration:

Greenhouses offer a living laboratory where children can explore various scientific concepts, including photosynthesis, water cycles, and plant anatomy. Through observation and experimentation, they develop critical thinking skills and a curiosity-driven approach to understanding the natural world.

3. **Seasonal Awareness:**

By gardening in a greenhouse, children learn about seasonal changes and how they affect plant growth. They discover the significance of factors like temperature, light exposure, and humidity, gaining an appreciation for the interconnectedness of environmental elements and plant development.

4. **Nutrition and Health:** Growing fruits, vegetables, and herbs in a greenhouse introduces children to the nutritional benefits of fresh, homegrown produce. They learn about the importance of a balanced diet and gain firsthand knowledge of where their food comes from, encouraging healthier eating habits.

5. **Environmental Stewardship:**

Greenhouse gardening instills a sense of environmental responsibility in children by highlighting the significance of sustainable practices, such as composting, water conservation, and organic gardening methods. They develop a deeper connection to nature and understand their role in preserving the planet for future generations.

6. Creativity and Expression:

Gardening allows children to express their creativity through designing and arranging plants in the greenhouse. Whether it's planning a themed garden, creating colorful arrangements, or experimenting with different plant combinations, they have the freedom to explore their artistic side while fostering a sense of ownership and pride in their work.

7. Emotional Well-being:

Engaging with nature has numerous mental health benefits for children, including stress reduction, improved mood, and increased self-esteem. Greenhouse gardening provides a tranquil and nurturing environment where children can unwind, connect with the natural world, and develop a sense of accomplishment as they watch their plants thrive and flourish.

8. Life Skills Development:
Gardening cultivates a range of valuable life skills in children, such as responsibility, patience, perseverance, and problem-solving. They learn the importance of commitment and consistency in caring for their plants, as well as resilience in the face of challenges like pests, diseases, and adverse weather conditions.

9. Family Bonding:
Greenhouse gardening offers an opportunity for meaningful family bonding as children and parents work together to nurture their plants and share the joys of gardening. It promotes communication, teamwork, and shared experiences, strengthening familial relationships and creating lasting memories.

10. Sense of Wonder and Discovery:

Above all, greenhouse gardening sparks a sense of wonder and discovery in children as they witness the miraculous transformation of tiny seeds into thriving plants. Each day brings new surprises and learning opportunities, fostering a lifelong love of nature and a sense of wonderment at the beauty and complexity of the natural world.

In summary, greenhouse gardening is an incredibly enriching and enjoyable activity for children, offering a holistic learning experience that combines scientific exploration, environmental stewardship, creativity, and emotional well-being. Through hands-on engagement with plants and nature, children develop valuable skills, deepen their understanding of the world around them, and cultivate a lifelong passion for gardening and environmental sustainability.

Safety guidelines for kids' greenhouse gardening

Ensuring safety is paramount when involving children in greenhouse gardening activities. Here's an extensive guide outlining safety guidelines to follow:

1. Supervision:

Always supervise children while they are in the greenhouse, especially younger ones. Designate an adult to oversee the gardening activities and ensure that children follow safety protocols.

2. Access Control:

Limit access to the greenhouse by installing childproof locks or latches on doors and windows. This prevents children from entering the greenhouse unsupervised and reduces the risk of accidents.

3. Structural Integrity:

Regularly inspect the greenhouse structure for any signs of damage or wear. Ensure that it is securely anchored to the ground and can withstand strong winds or inclement weather.

4. Temperature Control:
Monitor and regulate the temperature inside the greenhouse to prevent overheating or extreme cold. Install ventilation systems or shade cloth to control temperature fluctuations, especially during hot summer months.

5. Lighting Safety:
Be cautious with electrical lighting inside the greenhouse. Use waterproof, outdoor-rated fixtures and ensure that electrical cords are safely secured and out of reach of children to prevent tripping hazards or electrical shocks.

6. Chemical Storage:
Store fertilizers, pesticides, and other chemicals in locked cabinets or containers out of reach of children. Educate children about the potential dangers of these substances and

emphasize the importance of not touching or ingesting them.

7. Tool Safety:

Teach children how to safely use gardening tools and equipment, such as shovels, trowels, and pruners. Store sharp tools in a designated area when not in use and supervise children closely when they are handling them.

8. Plant Identification:

Teach children to identify poisonous plants and avoid touching or ingesting them. Label plants with their common and botanical names to facilitate learning and awareness.

9. Hygiene Practices:
Encourage children to wash their hands thoroughly after handling soil, plants, or gardening tools to prevent the spread of germs and reduce the risk of contamination.

10. Water Safety:
Be mindful of water sources inside the greenhouse, such as hoses, watering cans, or irrigation systems. Prevent children from playing or splashing in water containers to avoid slipping hazards and drowning risks.

11. Pest Management:
Implement non-toxic methods of pest control, such as handpicking insects or using organic insecticides, to minimize exposure to harmful chemicals. Help children learn how to identify

common garden pests and enlist their help in monitoring and managing pest populations.

12. Emergency Preparedness:
Have a first aid kit readily available in the greenhouse stocked with essential supplies for treating minor injuries. Enlighten children about what to do in case of emergencies, such as seeking medical help or contacting an adult.

13. Sun Protection:
Provide adequate sun protection for children working in the greenhouse, including sunscreen, hats, and lightweight clothing that covers exposed skin. Schedule gardening activities during cooler times of the day to minimize sun exposure and the risk of heat-related illnesses.

14. Respect for Wildlife:
Teach children to respect wildlife that may inhabit or visit the greenhouse, such as birds, insects, and small animals. Avoid disturbing

nests or habitats and encourage children to observe and appreciate the natural ecosystem.

15. Fire Safety:

Implement fire safety measures, such as installing smoke detectors and fire extinguishers, and have an evacuation plan in place in case of fire. Keep flammable materials away from heat sources and teach children how to respond calmly and safely in fire emergencies.

By following these safety guidelines, you can create a secure and nurturing environment for children to enjoy greenhouse gardening while minimizing risks and promoting a positive and educational experience. Remember that safety awareness and adult supervision are essential aspects of fostering a safe and enjoyable gardening environment for children.

Chapter 2: Getting Started with Greenhouse Gardening : Choosing the right greenhouse for kids

Embarking on the journey of greenhouse gardening with kids is an exciting and rewarding endeavor. One of the first steps is choosing the right greenhouse that suits both the needs of the children and the gardening objectives. Here's an extensive guide to getting started with selecting the perfect greenhouse for kids:

1. Consider Size and Space:

Determine how much space you have available for the greenhouse and consider the size of the structure accordingly. A smaller greenhouse is more manageable for kids and can provide an intimate setting for their gardening adventures, while larger greenhouses offer more room for experimentation and plant variety.

2. Choose a Suitable Design:

Greenhouses come in various designs, including freestanding, lean-to, and mini or tabletop models. Consider the layout of your garden or outdoor space and choose a design that complements the existing landscape while providing easy access for children to tend to their plants.

3. Select the Right Material:

Greenhouses are typically constructed from glass, polycarbonate, or plastic materials. Glass greenhouses offer excellent light transmission and durability but may pose safety concerns for children due to the risk of breakage. Polycarbonate or plastic greenhouses are safer alternatives that still provide adequate insulation and light diffusion.

4. Evaluate Ventilation Options:

Proper ventilation is important for regulating humidity and temperature levels inside the greenhouse. Look for models with adjustable vents, windows, or roof panels that allow for adequate airflow. This helps prevent overheating in warmer months and minimizes the risk of plant diseases.

5. Assess Durability and Stability:

Choose a greenhouse made from sturdy materials that can withstand outdoor elements and provide a stable environment for plants. Ensure that the greenhouse is securely anchored to the ground or a solid foundation to prevent tipping or damage during windy conditions.

6. Consider Assembly and Maintenance:

Opt for a greenhouse that is easy to assemble and requires minimal maintenance, especially when involving children in gardening activities. Look for models with simple, snap-together construction and removable panels for cleaning or repairs.

7. Explore Additional Features:

Some greenhouses come with additional features that enhance functionality and convenience. Consider features such as built-in shelves or benches for organizing pots and tools, integrated irrigation systems for efficient watering, or UV-resistant coatings for added durability.

8. Prioritize Safety Features:
Safety should be a top priority when selecting a greenhouse for kids. Choose models with rounded edges, smooth surfaces, and childproof latches or locks on doors and windows to prevent accidents. Avoid glass greenhouses or opt for tempered or safety glass to reduce the risk of breakage.

9. Involve Kids in the Decision-Making Process:
Encourage children to participate in choosing the greenhouse design and features, fostering a sense of ownership and excitement about their gardening project. Consider their preferences

and interests, such as favorite plants or colors, to create a space that reflects their personalities.

10. Budget Considerations

Determine your budget for the greenhouse project and explore options that fit within your financial constraints. While investing in a high-quality greenhouse may require a larger upfront cost, it can provide long-term benefits in terms of durability, functionality, and overall enjoyment for children.

11. Research and Compare Options:

Take the time to research different greenhouse models, read reviews, and compare features and prices from various manufacturers. Consider visiting garden centers or attending gardening expos to see different greenhouse designs firsthand and gather inspiration for your project.

12. Plan for Future Growth:

Anticipate the evolving needs of your greenhouse garden as children gain experience and interest in gardening. Choose a greenhouse that allows for expansion or customization, such as adding shelving, lighting, or additional ventilation, to accommodate growing plants and changing gardening goals.

By carefully considering these factors and involving children in the decision-making process, you can select a greenhouse that provides a safe, functional, and enjoyable space for kids to explore the wonders of gardening. Remember that the greenhouse is not just a structure but a gateway to endless learning opportunities and memorable experiences in the garden.

Setting up a greenhouse space

Setting up a greenhouse space for kids involves creating a welcoming and functional environment where they can learn, explore, and cultivate their love for gardening. Here's a detailed guide to setting up a greenhouse space that is safe, educational, and enjoyable for children:

1. Safety First:

Before setting up the greenhouse space, ensure that it is safe for children to use. Remove any sharp objects, chemicals, or potential hazards from the area. Check the greenhouse structure for stability and make any necessary repairs or reinforcements to prevent accidents.

2. Designate Gardening Zones:

Divide the greenhouse space into different gardening zones based on the types of plants or activities children will engage in. Create designated areas for planting beds, potting benches, seed starting stations, and storage for gardening tools and supplies.

3. Choose Child-Friendly Furniture:

Select child-sized gardening tools, pots, and furniture that are easy for kids to handle and manipulate. Opt for lightweight materials like plastic or wood and avoid heavy or cumbersome equipment that may be difficult for children to use safely.

4. Create Planting Beds:

Prepare raised planting beds or containers filled with nutrient-rich soil for growing plants. Arrange the beds in accessible locations within the greenhouse, ensuring that children can reach them easily without straining or overreaching.

5. Provide Adequate Lighting:

Ensure that the greenhouse space receives sufficient natural light for plant growth. Position planting beds and shelves near windows or skylights to maximize sunlight exposure. Supplement natural light with artificial grow lights if needed, especially during darker months or in shaded areas of the greenhouse.

6. Implement Irrigation Systems:

Set up a simple irrigation system to ensure consistent watering of plants and minimize the risk of over or under-watering. Install drip irrigation or soaker hoses that deliver water directly to the base of plants, reducing water waste and promoting healthy root development.

7. Organize Gardening Supplies:
Create a designated storage area for gardening supplies such as pots, potting soil, seeds, and fertilizers. Use shelves, bins, or cabinets to keep supplies organized and easily accessible for children to use during gardening activities.

8. Include Educational Resources:
Incorporate educational materials into the greenhouse space to enhance learning opportunities for children. Display books, posters, or charts that teach about plant life cycles, gardening techniques, and the importance of environmental stewardship.

9. Encourage Exploration and Creativity:
Create opportunities for children to explore and express their creativity within the

greenhouse space. Provide art supplies for decorating pots, markers for labeling plants, and materials for building trellises or garden structures.

10. Promote Sensory Engagement:
Incorporate sensory elements into the greenhouse design to engage children's senses and enhance their gardening experience. Include aromatic herbs, tactile textures, and colorful flowers that stimulate sight, smell, touch, and taste.

11. Establish a Gardening Routine:
Develop a regular gardening routine that children can follow to care for their plants and monitor their progress. Schedule time each week for watering, pruning, weeding, and harvesting, teaching children the importance of consistency and responsibility in gardening.

12. Create a Relaxation Space:

Dedicate a cozy corner of the greenhouse for relaxation and reflection. Include comfortable seating, cushions, and blankets where children can sit and observe their plants, read gardening books, or simply enjoy the peaceful ambiance of the greenhouse.

13. Encourage Collaboration and Sharing:

Foster a sense of community and collaboration among children by inviting them to share their gardening experiences and knowledge with each other. Arrange group activities such as planting parties, garden clean-up days, or harvest celebrations to promote teamwork and camaraderie.

14. Celebrate Achievements:

Recognize and celebrate children's gardening achievements by showcasing their plants, artwork, and accomplishments within the greenhouse space. Create a display area or bulletin board where children can proudly display photos, certificates, or awards earned through their gardening efforts.

15. Embrace Learning Opportunities:
Emphasize the importance of learning and experimentation in greenhouse gardening. Encourage children to ask questions, explore new ideas, and learn from their successes and failures. Use gardening as a platform for teaching valuable life skills such as patience, resilience, and problem-solving.

By following these guidelines, you can create a vibrant and engaging greenhouse space that ignites children's curiosity, nurtures their love for nature, and cultivates a lifelong passion for gardening. Remember to adapt the greenhouse setup to suit the unique interests, abilities, and preferences of the children involved, ensuring that they feel empowered and inspired to explore the wonders of the natural world.

Essential tools and supplies for kids' greenhouse gardening

Equipping kids with the right tools and supplies is essential for fostering a positive and productive greenhouse gardening experience. Here's a detailed overview of the essential items needed for kids' greenhouse gardening:

1. Child-Sized Gardening Tools:

Invest in high-quality, child-sized gardening tools that are safe, durable, and easy for kids to handle. Essential tools include:

   - Trowel: for digging small holes and transplanting seedlings.

   - Hand Fork: for loosening soil, removing weeds, and aerating the soil.

   - Hand Rake: for smoothing soil, leveling seed beds, and gathering debris.

   - Watering Can: with an average size and easy-to-use spout for watering plants.

   - Pruning Shears: with rounded tips and safety locks for trimming plants.

2. Planting Containers:

Provide a variety of planting containers suitable for different types of plants and gardening activities. Options include:

- Seedling Trays: for starting seeds indoors and transplanting seedlings.

- Pots and Planters: in various sizes and materials for growing herbs, vegetables, and flowers.

- Hanging Baskets: for suspending plants from overhead hooks or trellises to maximize space.

3. Potting Soil and Amendments:

Use high-quality potting soil or compost mixtures that are lightweight, well-draining, and rich in nutrients. Consider adding organic amendments such as compost, perlite, or vermiculite to improve soil structure and fertility.

4. Seeds and Seedlings:

Choose a selection of seeds and seedlings that are suitable for greenhouse growing and appeal to children's interests. Include a variety of vegetables, herbs, flowers, and ornamental plants to encourage diversity and experimentation.

5. Labels and Markers:

Provide labels and markers for identifying plants and keeping track of gardening activities. Use weatherproof labels or plant markers that withstand moisture and fading, and encourage children to label their pots or planting beds with the name and date of each plant.

6. Watering System:

Set up a simple watering system to ensure consistent moisture levels for plants. Options include:

- Spray Bottles: for misting seedlings and delicate plants.

- Watering Cans: with a rose attachment for gentle watering.

- Drip Irrigation: for automated watering of plants in pots or raised beds.

7. Fertilizers and Nutrients:

Use organic fertilizers or nutrient supplements to provide essential nutrients for plant growth.

Choose kid-safe formulas that are gentle on plants and environmentally friendly.

8. Protective Gear:

Equip children with protective gear to keep them safe while gardening. Essential items include:

   - Gloves: to protect hands from thorns, prickles, and soil.

   - Sun Hats: with wide brims or neck flaps to shade the face and neck from the sun.

   - Sunscreen: with a high SPF rating to safeguard exposed skin from harmful UV rays.

   - Gardening Aprons: with pockets for storing tools and supplies and protecting clothing from dirt and stains.

9. Educational Resources:

Provide books, posters, and other educational resources to enhance children's learning and engagement in greenhouse gardening. Choose age-appropriate materials that teach about plant life cycles, gardening techniques, and the importance of environmental stewardship.

10. Cleanup Supplies:

Keep the greenhouse space clean and organized with the following supplies:

- Brooms and Dustpans: for sweeping up debris and soil.
- Trash Bags: for collecting plant trimmings, weeds, and other garden waste.
- Cleaning Supplies: such as soap, water, and sponges for washing pots, trays, and tools.

11. Storage Solutions:

Provide storage containers, shelves, or cabinets for organizing gardening tools, supplies, and equipment. Encourage children to keep the greenhouse space tidy and accessible by returning tools and supplies to their designated storage areas after use.

12. Safety Equipment:

Ensure that children have access to safety equipment to prevent accidents and injuries. Essential safety items include:

- First Aid Kit: stocked with bandages, antiseptic wipes, tweezers, and other first aid essentials.

- Safety Glasses: for eye protection when using tools or handling soil and plants.

- Knee Pads: to cushion knees when kneeling or crouching while gardening.

By providing children with these essential tools and supplies, you can create a nurturing and empowering environment for greenhouse gardening that promotes learning, creativity, and hands-on exploration. Encourage children to take ownership of their gardening projects and instill a sense of pride and responsibility in caring for their plants and the natural world.

Chapter 3: Selecting Plants for the Greenhouse : Easy-to-grow plants for kids

Selecting plants for a kids' greenhouse involves choosing varieties that are easy to grow, visually appealing, and engaging for children. Here's a detailed overview of some easy-to-grow plants that are perfect for kids' greenhouse gardening:

1. Herbs:

Herbs are ideal for kids' greenhouse gardening because they are easy to grow, aromatic, and offer sensory exploration. Popular herbs to grow include:

- Basil: with its fragrant leaves and quick growth.

- Mint: with its refreshing scent and resilience.

- Chives: with their mild onion flavor and attractive flowers.

- Thyme: with its tiny leaves and drought tolerance.

- Parsley: with its curly or flat leaves and versatility in cooking.

2. Vegetables:

Growing vegetables in the greenhouse teaches children about healthy eating and provides a sense of accomplishment. Easy-to-grow vegetables include:

- Cherry Tomatoes: with their sweet flavor and prolific production.

- Lettuce: with its fast growth and variety of leaf shapes and colors.

- Radishes: with their quick turnaround from seed to harvest.

- Carrots: with their crunchy texture and vibrant colors.

- Peas: with their climbing vines and sweet pods.

3. Flowers:

Flowers add beauty and color to the greenhouse while attracting pollinators and beneficial insects. Easy-to-grow flowers for kids include:

- Marigolds: with their bright orange and yellow blooms.

- Sunflowers: with their towering stems and cheerful faces.

- Nasturtiums: with their edible flowers and trailing vines.

- Zinnias: with their bold colors and long-lasting blooms.

- Cosmos: with their delicate petals and airy foliage.

4. Fruits:

Growing fruits in the greenhouse introduces children to the joys of harvesting their own food. Easy-to-grow fruit options include:

- Strawberries: with their sweet berries and compact growth habit.

- Blueberries: with their antioxidant-rich fruit and colorful foliage.

- Raspberries: with their tart berries and vigorous growth.

- Dwarf Citrus Trees: with their fragrant flowers and miniature fruit.

- Dwarf Apple or Pear Trees: with their manageable size and abundant harvests.

5. Succulents and Cacti:

Succulents and cacti are low-maintenance plants that thrive in the warm, dry conditions of the greenhouse. Children can enjoy their unique shapes and textures without worrying about frequent watering. Popular varieties include:

- Aloe Vera: with its spiky leaves and soothing gel.

- Jade Plant: with its fleshy leaves and easy propagation.

- Echeveria: with its rosette-shaped foliage and vibrant colors.

- Cactus: with its prickly stems and diverse shapes and sizes.

- Haworthia: with its striped or spotted leaves and compact growth habit.

6. Microgreens:

Microgreens are nutritious and easy to grow indoors, making them perfect for kids' greenhouse gardening. Children can watch them sprout and harvest them in just a few weeks. Common microgreens include:

- Pea Shoots: with their tender stems and sweet flavor.

- Radish Sprouts: with their peppery taste and vibrant colors.

- Sunflower Shoots: with their nutty flavor and crunchy texture.

- Beet Greens: with their earthy flavor and colorful stems.

7. Air Purifying Plants:

Introducing air-purifying plants into the greenhouse not only improves air quality but also adds visual interest and educational value. Easy-to-grow air-purifying plants include:

- Spider Plant: with its arching foliage and spider-like offshoots.

- Snake Plant: with its upright leaves and low-maintenance care.

- Peace Lily: with its white flowers and tolerance for low light.

- Pothos: with its trailing vines and ability to thrive in various conditions.

8. Culinary Projects:

Engage children in fun and educational culinary projects by growing plants that can be used in cooking or crafting. Consider:

- Wheatgrass: for juicing or decorating.

- Edible Flowers: such as pansies or violets, for garnishing salads or desserts.

- Ginger or Turmeric: for growing and harvesting rhizomes to use in cooking or tea.

When selecting plants for kids' greenhouse gardening, consider factors such as growth rate, care requirements, and suitability for the greenhouse environment. Choose a mix of plants that appeal to children's interests and offer opportunities for hands-on learning, sensory exploration, and creative expression. By choosing the right selection of plants, kids can experience the satisfaction and joy of watching their garden thrive and grow.

Vegetables, herbs, flowers, and fruits suitable for greenhouse gardening

Engaging kids in greenhouse gardening with a variety of plants can foster their curiosity, teach them about nature, and encourage healthy eating habits. Here's an extensive guide to vegetables, herbs, flowers, and fruits suitable for kids' greenhouse gardening:

Vegetables:

1. Tomatoes: Cherry tomatoes are prolific producers and grow well in containers. They offer sweet, bite-sized fruits that kids can snack on straight from the vine.

2. Lettuce: Lettuce is easy to grow and provides a quick harvest. Kids can enjoy watching the leaves grow and use them in salads or sandwiches.

3. Radishes: Radishes have a short growing season and are ready to harvest in just a few weeks. They come in various colors and shapes, making them visually appealing to kids.

4. Carrots: Carrots are fun to grow because kids can harvest them by pulling them straight from the soil. They come in different colors, including orange, purple, and yellow, adding excitement to the garden.

5. Peas: Peas are climbing plants that kids can train to grow trellises or stakes. They produce sweet pods that are fun to pick and eat fresh from the garden.

Herbs:
1. Basil: Basil is a versatile herb with a fragrant aroma and vibrant flavor. Kids can use it in cooking, make pesto, or simply enjoy its fresh leaves in salads or sandwiches.

2. Mint: Mint is easy to grow and comes in various flavors, including peppermint and spearmint. Kids can use it to make refreshing teas, lemonades, or flavored water.

3. Chives: Chives have mild onion flavor and produce attractive purple flowers. Kids can snip the leaves to use as a garnish or flavoring in dishes like soups, omelets, or baked potatoes.

4. Thyme: Thyme is a hardy herb that adds savory flavor to dishes. Kids can use it to season meats, vegetables, or homemade sauces.

5. Parsley: Parsley is a versatile herb with curly or flat leaves. Kids can use it to garnish dishes, add flavor to salads, or make homemade tabbouleh.

Flowers:
1. Marigolds: Marigolds are easy-to-grow flowers with bright orange or yellow blooms. They attract beneficial insects to the garden

and can be used as companion plants to repel pests.

2. Sunflowers: Sunflowers are tall, cheerful flowers that kids love to grow. They come in various sizes and colors and produce edible seeds that can be roasted and eaten.

3. Nasturtiums: Nasturtiums have edible flowers and peppery leaves that kids can add to salads or sandwiches. They come in a range of colors and have a trailing habit, making them ideal for hanging baskets or containers.

4. Zinnias: Zinnias are colorful, easy-to-grow flowers that bloom in a wide range of hues. They attract butterflies to the garden and make lovely cut flowers for arrangements.

5. Cosmos: Cosmos are low-maintenance flowers with delicate petals and fern-like foliage. They come in shades of pink, purple, and white and attract pollinators like bees and butterflies.

Fruits:

1. **Strawberries:** Strawberries are delicious, easy-to-grow fruits that kids can harvest and eat fresh from the garden. They come in various sizes and colors and can be grown in containers or hanging baskets.

2. **Blueberries:** Blueberries are antioxidant-rich fruits that thrive in acidic soil. Kids can enjoy watching the berries ripen and picking them for snacks or baking.

3. **Raspberries:** Raspberries are sweet, juicy fruits that grow on thorny canes. Kids can harvest them by gently pulling them from the plant and enjoy them fresh or in jams, pies, or smoothies.

4. **Dwarf Citrus Trees:** Dwarf citrus trees, such as lemons, limes, or oranges, are compact

and manageable for greenhouse gardening. Kids can watch the trees bloom and produce fragrant fruits throughout the year.

5. Dwarf Apple or Pear Trees: Dwarf apple or pear trees are perfect for greenhouse gardening, providing a mini orchard experience for kids. They produce crisp, flavorful fruits that can be eaten fresh or used in cooking and baking.

By including a variety of vegetables, herbs, flowers, and fruits in kids' greenhouse gardening, you can create a diverse and engaging learning environment that sparks their curiosity, teaches them valuable skills, and fosters a lifelong love of gardening and nature. Encourage children to actively participate in caring for their plants, harvesting their produce, and exploring the wonders of the natural world.

Planning and designing a kid-friendly greenhouse garden

Designing a kid-friendly greenhouse garden involves creating a space that is safe, engaging, and educational for children to explore and learn about gardening. Here's an extensive guide to planning and designing a greenhouse garden specifically with kids in mind:

1. Safety Considerations

- Prioritize safety by selecting child-friendly materials and eliminating potential hazards.
- Choose plants that are non-toxic and avoid thorny or prickly varieties.
- Install childproof locks on doors and windows to prevent accidents.
- Ensure pathways are clear and free of tripping hazards.

2. Accessible Layout:

- Design the greenhouse with pathways wide enough for children to navigate comfortably.

- Arrange planting beds and containers at a child-friendly height, allowing easy access for planting, watering, and harvesting.

- Create designated areas for different gardening activities, such as planting beds, potting benches, and relaxation spaces.

3. Engaging Themes:

- Incorporate fun and engaging themes into the greenhouse design to capture children's imagination.

- Consider themes like a fairy garden, a pizza garden (with herbs and vegetables for making pizzas), or a sensory garden with plants that appeal to all five senses.

4. Interactive Elements:

- Include interactive elements that encourage hands-on exploration and learning.

- Install magnifying glasses or microscopes for examining plant parts and insects up close.

- Set up a weather station to track temperature, humidity, and rainfall.

- Provide educational signage or labels for plants, teaching children about their names, growth habits, and care requirements.

5. Sensory Garden Features:

- Incorporate plants with different textures, colors, and scents to stimulate children's senses.
- Include aromatic herbs like mint, lavender, and rosemary for smelling.
- Plant fuzzy lamb's ear or soft ferns for touching.
- Add colorful flowers like marigolds, zinnias, and sunflowers for visual interest.

6. Child-Sized Furniture and Tools:

- Provide child-sized gardening tools and furniture that are easy for kids to handle.
- Choose lightweight materials like plastic or wood and ensure that tools have rounded edges and comfortable grips.
- Include child-sized tables, chairs, and benches for potting, crafting, and relaxation.

7. Container Gardening:

- Incorporate container gardening to maximize space and flexibility in the greenhouse.

- Use colorful pots, baskets, and containers to add visual interest and appeal to children.

- Plant a variety of herbs, vegetables, and flowers in containers that can be easily moved or rearranged.

8. Vertical Gardening:

- Utilize vertical space for growing plants to maximize growing area.

- Install trellises, hanging baskets, or vertical planters for climbing plants like peas, beans, or cucumbers.

- Create living walls or vertical gardens with ferns, succulent or trailing plants.

9. Water Features:

- Incorporate child-safe water features like small fountains, birdbaths, or shallow ponds to attract wildlife and add tranquility to the greenhouse.

- Teach children about the importance of water conservation and provide opportunities for them to participate in watering plants.

10. Creative Play Areas:

- Designate areas for creative play and exploration within the greenhouse.

- Set up a mud kitchen or sensory table for messy play with soil, sand, and water.

- Create art stations with supplies for drawing, painting, or crafting with natural materials.

11. Educational Resources:

- Provide books, posters, and educational materials about plants, gardening, and nature.

- Incorporate interactive learning activities like scavenger hunts, plant identification games, or nature journals.

12. Flexible Spaces:

- Design the greenhouse with flexibility in mind to accommodate children's changing interests and needs.

- Include movable furniture, modular planters, and adaptable layouts that can be easily adjusted or reconfigured over time.

13. Child-Centric Events and Activities:

- Organize regular events and activities tailored to children's interests and abilities.

- Host gardening workshops, seed-starting parties, or harvest celebrations to engage children in hands-on learning and social interaction.

14. Safety Guidelines and Rules

- Establish clear safety guidelines and rules for children to follow while in the greenhouse.

- Educate children about potential hazards and teach them proper gardening techniques and practices.

- Supervise children closely and provide guidance and support as needed.

15. Encourage Creativity and Ownership:

- Empower children to take ownership of their greenhouse garden by involving them in planning, planting, and caring for their plants.

- Encourage creativity and self-expression through gardening projects, art activities, and personalization of the greenhouse space.

By incorporating these elements into the design of a kid-friendly greenhouse garden, you can create a nurturing and inspiring environment that fosters children's curiosity, creativity, and connection to nature. Encourage children to explore, experiment, and learn at their own pace while cultivating a lifelong love of gardening and environmental stewardship.

Chapter 4: Greenhouse Gardening Practical Activities

Greenhouse gardening practical activities for kids refer to hands-on, experiential learning experiences specifically designed for children within the context of greenhouse gardening. These activities engage children in various gardening tasks, experiments, and explorations that foster learning, skill development, and enjoyment in a greenhouse environment. Below are some exciting practicals and activities kids can try out.

Hands-on experiments and projects

Hands-on experiments and projects are invaluable components of greenhouse gardening for kids, offering engaging opportunities for learning, exploration, and discovery. These activities allow children to observe, investigate, and interact with plants and the natural world in a hands-on manner, fostering curiosity, critical thinking, and scientific inquiry. Here's an extensive look at hands-on experiments and projects suitable for kids in greenhouse gardening:

1. Seed Germination Experiment:
   -Objective: To observe and document the process of seed germination.
   -Materials: Seeds (e.g., beans, peas, sunflowers), potting soil, containers, water.

-Procedure: Plant seeds in separate containers filled with moist soil. Keep one container in the greenhouse and another in a dark, cool place. Observe and compare the germination rates, seedling growth, and plant development over time.

2. Soil Investigation:

- Objective: To explore the properties of soil and understand its importance for plant growth.

- Materials: Soil samples from different locations (e.g., garden soil, potting mix, compost), magnifying glasses, pH test kits, water.

- Procedure: Collect soil samples from various areas and examine their texture, color, and composition. Test the pH levels of each soil sample and discuss how soil pH affects plant health and nutrient availability.

3. Watering Experiment:

- Objective: To investigate the effects of different watering regimes on plant growth.

- Materials: Identical plant pots, potting soil, seeds or seedlings, watering cans, measuring cups.

- Procedure: Divide plants into groups and water each group with different amounts of water (e.g., daily watering, alternate-day watering, weekly watering). Measure and record plant growth, leaf color, and soil moisture levels over time to determine the optimal watering frequency for healthy plant growth.

4. Light Exposure Study:
   - Objective: To study the effects of light exposure on plant growth and development.

- Materials: Identical plant pots, potting soil, seeds or seedlings, grow lights or sunlight, light meter.

- Procedure: Place plants in different locations within the greenhouse, varying the amount of light exposure they receive (e.g., full sun, partial shade, low light). Measure and record plant growth, leaf size, and stem elongation to analyze the effects of light intensity on photosynthesis and plant morphology.

5. Companion Planting Project:

- Objective: To explore the concept of companion planting and its benefits for plant health and productivity.

- Materials: Seeds or seedlings of compatible plant species, planting containers or garden beds, gardening tools.

- Procedure: Plant different combinations of companion plants together in containers or garden beds based on their compatibility and mutual benefits (e.g., pest control, nutrient sharing). Observe and document the interactions between companion plants and evaluate their growth, yield, and overall health.

6. Pollination Observation:
- Objective: To observe the process of pollination and its importance for plant reproduction.

- Materials: Flowers with open blooms, magnifying glasses, observation journals.

- Procedure: Select flowers with visible reproductive structures (e.g., stamens, pistils) and observe pollinators (e.g., bees, butterflies) visiting the flowers. Document the pollination process, including pollen transfer and flower visitation patterns, and discuss the role of pollinators in plant reproduction and fruit formation.

7. Propagation Project:

- Objective: To learn about plant propagation techniques and practice propagating new plants.

- Materials: Pruning shears, rooting hormone, potting soil, containers, plant cuttings or divisions.

- Procedure: Select plants suitable for propagation (e.g., herbs, succulents) and take cuttings or divisions from healthy parent plants. Apply rooting hormone to the cut ends and plant them in containers filled with moist soil. Monitor the cuttings or divisions for root development and transplant them into larger pots once roots have formed.

8. Seasonal Planting Calendar:

-Objective: To create a seasonal planting calendar based on plant growth requirements and climate conditions.

- Materials: Garden planner or calendar, seed packets or plant catalogs, markers, stickers.

70

- Procedure: Research optimal planting times for different crops based on local climate conditions and frost dates. Use a calendar or planner to schedule planting dates, transplanting dates, and harvest times for each crop. Decorate the calendar with stickers or drawings to represent each plant and its growth stages.

9. Herb Garden Design Project:

- Objective: To design and plan a herb garden layout based on plant compatibility and growing conditions.

- Materials: Graph paper, colored pencils or markers, ruler, seed packets or plant catalogs.

- Procedure: Draw a scale model of the greenhouse space and design a herb garden layout, considering factors such as sunlight exposure, water availability, and plant height. Research companion planting combinations and arrange herbs in groupings based on their compatibility and complementary growth habits.

10. Harvest Celebration:

- Objective: To celebrate the culmination of greenhouse gardening efforts and enjoy the fruits of labor.

- Materials: Harvested fruits, vegetables, herbs, flowers, picnic supplies.

- Procedure: Organize a harvest celebration in the greenhouse or outdoor garden area to commemorate the end of the growing season. Invite friends and family to share in the harvest and enjoy a picnic or potluck meal featuring freshly harvested produce. Take photos and create a scrapbook or memory book to document the harvest celebration.

These hands-on experiments and projects provide children with meaningful opportunities to engage with greenhouse gardening concepts, develop scientific inquiry skills, and deepen their understanding of plants and nature.

Learning about ecosystems, pollination, and beneficial insects through practicals

Learning about ecosystems, pollination, and beneficial insects through practical activities in greenhouse gardening provides children with valuable insights into the interconnectedness of living organisms and the importance of biodiversity in sustaining healthy ecosystems. Here's a detailed exploration of how kids can learn about these concepts through hands-on experiences:

1. Exploring Ecosystems:

- Objective: To understand the concept of ecosystems and the relationships between living organisms and their environment.

- Practical Activities:

  - Habitat Exploration: Take children on a guided tour of the greenhouse to observe different habitats within the ecosystem, such as soil, plants, and microorganisms. Discuss the roles of producers, consumers, and decomposers in the ecosystem.

- Food Web Activity: Create a food web diagram to illustrate the interconnected relationships between plants, animals, and other organisms in the greenhouse ecosystem. Discuss the flow of energy and nutrients through the food chain.

- Water Cycle Demonstration: Set up a simple water cycle demonstration using containers of water, heat sources, and plastic wrap to simulate evaporation, condensation, and precipitation. Discuss the importance of water for plant growth and ecosystem health.

2. Studying Pollination:

-Objective: To learn about the process of pollination and the role of pollinators in plant reproduction.

- Practical Activities:

- Pollinator Observation: Encourage children to observe pollinators such as bees, butterflies, and hummingbirds visiting flowers in the greenhouse. Provide magnifying glasses and observation journals for documenting pollinator behavior and flower visitation patterns.

- Pollination Experiment: Conduct a pollination experiment using flowers with visible reproductive structures (e.g., stamens, pistils) and different pollination methods (e.g., self-pollination, cross-pollination). Observe and compare the effects of pollination on fruit formation and seed production.

- Pollinator Garden Planting: Create a pollinator-friendly garden in the greenhouse by planting flowers that attract bees, butterflies, and other pollinators. Discuss the importance of providing habitat and food sources for pollinators to support biodiversity and ecosystem resilience.

3. Identifying Beneficial Insects:

- Objective: To recognize the importance of beneficial insects in controlling pests and promoting plant health.

- Practical Activities:

- Insect Observation: Set up insect traps or sticky traps in the greenhouse to collect and identify insects. Teach children to distinguish between beneficial insects (e.g., ladybugs, lacewings, parasitic wasps) and harmful pests (e.g., aphids, caterpillars).

- Insect Identification Guide: Create an insect identification guide with pictures and descriptions of common beneficial insects found in the greenhouse. Discuss the roles of beneficial insects in pest control and integrated pest management strategies.

- Beneficial Insect Release: Purchase or rear beneficial insects (e.g., ladybugs, praying mantises) and release them into the greenhouse to control pest populations naturally. Monitor and observe the effects of beneficial insect predation on pest populations over time.

4. Creating Habitat Enhancements:

- Objective: To provide habitat enhancements to support beneficial insects and other native wildlife in the greenhouse ecosystem.

- Practical Activities:

  - Insect Hotels: Build insect hotels or bug houses using recycled materials such as wood, bamboo, and cardboard. Place the insect hotels in strategic locations within the greenhouse to provide nesting sites and shelter for beneficial insects.

  - Butterfly Gardens: Plant butterfly-attracting flowers such as milkweed, coneflowers, and butterfly bush to create a butterfly garden in the greenhouse. Provide shallow dishes of water with rocks for butterflies to drink from and bask in the sun.

  - Bird Feeders and Baths: Install bird feeders and baths outside the greenhouse to attract birds that feed on insect pests and contribute to ecosystem balance. Encourage children to observe and identify bird species visiting the feeders and baths.

Through these practical activities, children gain a deeper appreciation for the complexity and diversity of ecosystems, the essential role of pollinators in plant reproduction, and the importance of beneficial insects in maintaining ecological balance. By engaging in hands-on learning experiences, children develop a greater understanding of the natural world and become advocates for biodiversity conservation and environmental stewardship.

Keeping a garden journal and recording observations

Keeping a garden journal and recording observations is a valuable practice for children engaged in greenhouse gardening. It provides them with a way to document their experiences, track plant growth, and reflect on their observations over time. Here's a detailed exploration of how children can keep a garden journal and record their observations in the greenhouse:

1. Setting Up the Garden Journal:
 - Materials: Notebook or journal, pens or pencils, colored markers or pencils, ruler, camera (optional).
 - Introduction: Begin by introducing children to the concept of a garden journal and its purpose. Explain that the journal will serve as a record of their greenhouse gardening experiences, including observations, experiments, and reflections.

- Personalization: Encourage children to personalize their garden journals by decorating the covers with drawings, stickers, or photographs of plants. This helps create a sense of ownership and pride in their journal.

2. Recording Observations:
 - Daily Entries: Encourage children to make daily entries in their garden journals, recording observations of plant growth, changes in weather, and any notable events or discoveries in the greenhouse.
 - Observation Prompts: Provide children with observation prompts to guide their journal entries. Prompts may include questions such as:
   - What do you notice about the plants today?
   - Are there any new flowers, buds, or fruits?
   - What is the weather like inside the greenhouse?
   - Did you see any insects or wildlife in the greenhouse?

- Sketches and Diagrams: Encourage children to draw sketches or diagrams of plants, flowers, and insects they observe in the greenhouse. Drawing helps improve observation skills and allows children to express themselves creatively.

3. Documenting Plant Growth:
   - Measurements: Have children measure and record the height, width, and other dimensions

of plants at regular intervals. Use a ruler or measuring tape to accurately record plant growth over time.

- Photographs: Take photographs of plants at different stages of growth and include them in the garden journal. Children can use the photographs to compare and contrast changes in plant appearance over time.

4. Recording Experiments and Projects:

- Experiment Logs: If children conduct experiments or projects in the greenhouse, have them record detailed logs of their procedures, observations, and results in the garden journal. This helps reinforce the scientific method and critical thinking skills.

- Project Reflections: Encourage children to reflect on their experiments and projects, discussing what they learned, any unexpected outcomes, and ideas for future investigations.

5. Seasonal Observations:

- Seasonal Changes: Have children observe and record seasonal changes in the greenhouse throughout the year. Document the emergence of new growth in spring, the abundance of flowers and fruits in summer, the changing colors of leaves in fall, and the dormancy of plants in winter.

- Seasonal Activities: Include seasonal activities and traditions in the garden journal, such as planting seeds in spring, harvesting fruits and vegetables in summer, and decorating the greenhouse for holidays in winter.

6. Reflections and Goals:

- Reflective Writing: Encourage children to write reflective entries in their garden journals, discussing their thoughts, feelings, and experiences related to greenhouse gardening. Prompt them to reflect on what they enjoyed, what they found challenging, and how they can improve in the future.

- Setting Goals: Have children set goals for their greenhouse gardening activities and record them in their journals. Goals may include growing specific plants, experimenting with new techniques, or attracting beneficial insects to the greenhouse.

7. Sharing and Celebrating:

- Sharing Experiences: Provide opportunities for children to share their garden journal entries with peers, family members, or educators. Encourage them to discuss their observations, discoveries, and insights with others.

- Celebrating Achievements: Celebrate children's achievements in greenhouse gardening by acknowledging their efforts and progress recorded in their garden journals. Host a journal sharing session or showcase where children can display their journals and discuss their experiences with others.

8. Long-Term Engagement:

- Continued Practice: Encourage children to continue keeping their garden journals as they engage in greenhouse gardening activities over time. Emphasize the importance of regular observation and documentation for deepening their understanding of plants and nature.

- Reflection and Growth: Encourage children to review their earlier journal entries periodically and reflect on how their knowledge, skills, and observations have evolved over time. This helps foster a sense of growth and progress in their greenhouse gardening journey.

By keeping a garden journal and recording their observations in the greenhouse, children develop important skills in observation, documentation, reflection, and goal-setting. They gain a deeper understanding of plants and ecosystems, cultivate a lifelong appreciation for nature, and create a meaningful record of their greenhouse gardening experiences.

Chapter 5: Fun Activities and Games for Greenhouse Gardening

Fun activities and games for greenhouse gardening are interactive and engaging experiences designed to make gardening enjoyable and educational for children. These activities aim to foster a love for plants, nature, and gardening while providing opportunities for hands-on learning and creative expression.

Fun activities and games in greenhouse gardening can include a variety of playful tasks, challenges, and exploration opportunities tailored to the interests and abilities of children. Examples include plant identification games, seed sorting contests, garden scavenger hunts, and plant-themed crafts. By participating in these activities, children can develop important gardening skills, such as planting, watering, and caring for plants, while also cultivating a deeper understanding of the natural world and the importance of environmental stewardship.

Overall, fun activities and games for greenhouse gardening offer children a joyful and enriching way to connect with nature and nurture their curiosity and creativity.

Garden-themed crafts and DIY projects

Garden-themed crafts and DIY projects are fantastic ways to engage kids in greenhouse gardening while sparking their creativity and imagination. These activities allow children to express themselves artistically while learning about plants and the natural world. Here are some fun garden-themed craft ideas for kids:

1. Seed Bombs:
   - Mix together clay, compost, and wildflower seeds to create seed bombs.
   - Show kids how to roll the mixture into small balls and let them dry.
   - Once dry, kids can throw the seed bombs into areas of the garden or outdoor spaces to promote wildflower growth.

2. Pressed Flower Art:
   - Collect flowers and leaves from the garden and press them between the pages of heavy books for a few days.

- Once dried, arrange the pressed flowers and leaves on paper or cardstock to create beautiful artwork.

- Encourage kids to use their imagination to design scenes or patterns with the pressed flowers.

3. Plant Markers:

- Gather smooth rocks or wooden craft sticks from the garden or craft store.

- Provide paint, markers, or permanent pens for kids to decorate the rocks or sticks with the names or pictures of different plants.

- Once decorated and dried, use the plant markers to label pots or garden beds in the greenhouse.

4. Terrariums:

- Gather glass containers or jars, potting soil, small plants, and decorative elements like rocks or figurines.

- Show kids how to layer the bottom of the container with rocks for drainage, followed by a layer of soil.

- Let kids plant small succulents or ferns in the soil and decorate the terrarium with rocks, pebbles, or miniature accessories.

5. Recycled Planters:

- Collect recyclable materials like plastic bottles, tin cans, or yogurt containers.

- Help kids cut, decorate, and repurpose these materials into unique planters for their greenhouse plants.

- Encourage creativity by using paint, stickers, or markers to personalize the recycled planters.

6. Nature Collages:

- Go on a nature walk to collect leaves, flowers, seeds, and other natural materials.

- Provide cardboard or paper as a base for the collage.

- Encourage kids to arrange and glue the collected items onto the cardboard to create colorful and textured nature collages.

7. Herb Sachets:

- Gather dried herbs from the garden, such as lavender, rosemary, or mint.

- Provide small fabric squares or sachet bags.

- Let kids fill the fabric squares with a mixture of dried herbs and tie them closed to create aromatic herb sachets.

These garden-themed crafts and DIY projects not only inspire creativity and hands-on exploration but also reinforce the connection between children and the natural world.

Nature-inspired games and activities for kids

Nature-inspired games and activities for kids in greenhouse gardening provide exciting opportunities to engage with the natural world while learning about plants and gardening. These activities encourage exploration, observation, and creativity, making greenhouse gardening a fun and educational experience for children. Here are some delightful nature-inspired games and activities for kids:

1. Plant Bingo:
    - Create bingo cards featuring pictures or names of plants commonly found in the greenhouse.
    - Give each kid a bingo card and a marker.
    - As they explore the greenhouse, kids mark off the plants on their bingo cards when they find them.

- The first kid to complete a row, column, or diagonal shouts "Bingo!" and wins a small prize.

2. Bug Hunt:
 - Provide magnifying glasses and bug identification charts.
 - Encourage kids to search for insects and other small creatures living in the greenhouse.
 - Help them identify and learn about the different bugs they find, discussing their characteristics and roles in the ecosystem.

3. Plant Pictionary:
 - Divide kids into teams and provide drawing materials.
 - Assign each team a plant or gardening-related word or phrase (e.g., sunflower, watering can).
 - One member of each team draws a picture of the word or phrase while the rest of the team guesses what it is.

- The team that guesses correctly earns a point, and play continues with new words or phrases.

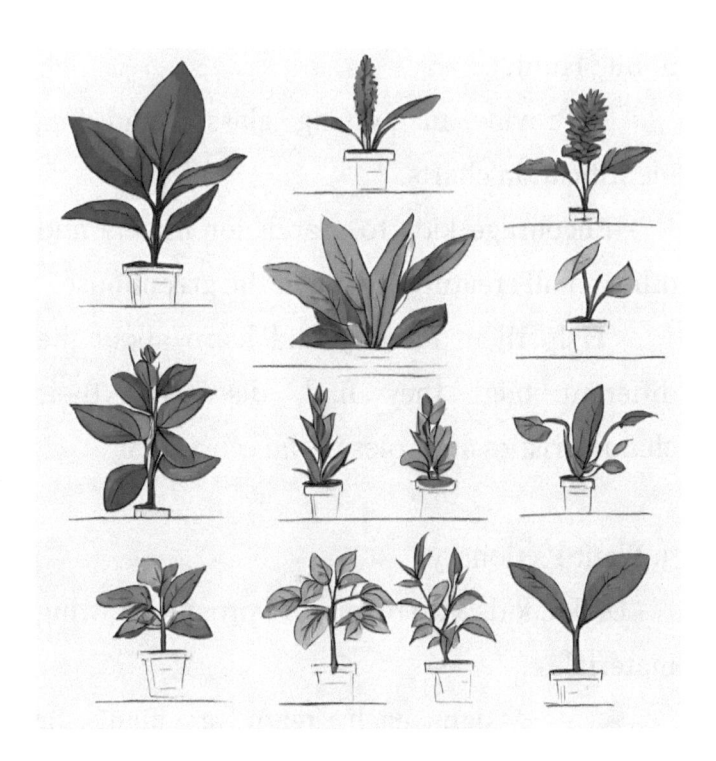

4. Sensory Garden Exploration:
    - Set up a sensory garden area in the greenhouse with plants that engage the senses, such as fragrant herbs, fuzzy leaves, or colorful flowers.

96

- Encourage kids to explore the sensory garden by touching, smelling, and observing the different plants.

- Ask them to describe their sensory experiences and how each plant makes them feel.

5. Plant Relay Race:

- Set up a relay race course with designated starting and finishing lines.

- Place pots or trays of small plants at the starting line.

- Divide kids into teams and give each team a small watering can.

- On "Go," the first player from each team races to the starting line, waters a plant, and returns to tag the next player.

- The first team to water all their plants and cross the finish line wins the race.

6. Leaf Rubbings:

- Collect a variety of leaves from different plants in the greenhouse.

- Provide paper and crayons or pencils.

- Show kids how to place a leaf under the paper and gently rub the crayon or pencil over it to create a leaf rubbing.

- Encourage them to experiment with different colors and types of leaves to create unique artworks.

7. Garden Story Stones:

- Collect smooth stones from the garden or craft store.

- Use paint or permanent markers to decorate the stones with pictures of plants, animals, and gardening tools.

- Encourage kids to use the story stones to create imaginative stories or plays about the garden and its inhabitants.

These nature-inspired games and activities not only make greenhouse gardening enjoyable for kids but also foster a deeper connection to the natural world. By engaging in these activities, children can develop their observation skills, creativity, and appreciation for the wonders of nature while having fun in the greenhouse.

Hosting a greenhouse gardening party for friends and family

Hosting a greenhouse gardening party for friends and family is an engaging and educational way to share the joys of gardening while creating lasting memories together. Here's how to plan and host a fun-filled greenhouse gardening party that everyone will enjoy:

1. Invitations and Theme:
   - Send out invitations to friends and family, inviting them to join in the greenhouse gardening party.
   - Choose a theme for the party, such as "Greenhouse Garden Gathering" or "Blooming Bash," and incorporate it into the invitations and decorations.

2. Greenhouse Tour and Introduction:

- Start the party with a guided tour of the greenhouse, led by the host or an experienced gardener.

- Introduce guests to the different plants, flowers, and herbs growing in the greenhouse, highlighting their unique features and growing requirements.

3. Hands-on Activities:

- Plan a variety of hands-on activities for guests to participate in, such as planting seeds, repotting plants, or harvesting herbs and vegetables.

- Set up stations with all the necessary supplies and instructions for each activity, ensuring that guests of all ages can get involved.

4. Garden Games and Challenges:

- Organize garden-themed games and challenges to add excitement to the party.

- Consider activities like a plant identification scavenger hunt, a seedling relay race, or a gardening trivia quiz.

- Offer small prizes or awards for winners to make the games even more enjoyable.

5. DIY Projects and Crafts:

- Provide materials for guests to create their own garden-themed crafts or DIY projects.

- Ideas include decorating plant pots, making seed bombs, or crafting plant markers.

- Encourage creativity and experimentation, allowing guests to take home their creations as souvenirs.

6. Refreshments and Snacks:
   - Offer refreshments and snacks inspired by the garden theme, such as herbal teas, fresh fruit platters, or vegetable crudités with dips.

- Consider incorporating edible flowers or herbs into the menu for added flair and flavor.

7. Garden Party Decorations:
    - Decorate the greenhouse with garden-themed decorations, such as bunting, banners, and potted plants.

- Use natural materials like twine, straw, and dried flowers to create rustic and whimsical accents.

- Set up seating areas with cushions or benches where guests can relax and enjoy the ambiance.

8. Take-home Gifts and Favors:
   - Provide guests with take-home gifts or favors to thank them for attending the party.
   - Ideas include potted plants, packets of seeds, gardening tools, or handmade crafts.
   - Personalize the gifts with tags or labels featuring the party theme for an extra special touch.

By hosting a greenhouse gardening party for friends and family, you can create a fun and memorable experience that celebrates the joys of gardening and fosters a love for nature. With hands-on activities, games, crafts, and refreshments, everyone can enjoy a day of creativity, learning, and connection in the beautiful surroundings of the greenhouse.

Chapter 6: Planting and Propagating

Planting and propagating are fundamental aspects of greenhouse gardening for kids, providing hands-on opportunities to nurture plants, learn about their life cycles, and experience the joys of watching seeds sprout and cuttings root. Here's an exploration of how children can engage in planting and propagating activities in the greenhouse:

1. Selecting Plants:
   - Seed Selection: Introduce children to a variety of seeds for plants that are suitable for greenhouse growing. Choose seeds of vegetables, herbs, flowers, and fruits that are easy to grow and well-suited to the greenhouse environment.

   3. Caring for Seedlings:
   - Watering: Instruct children on the importance of keeping seedlings consistently moist but not waterlogged. Teach them how to

water seedlings gently to avoid disturbing the soil or damaging delicate stems.

- Light Requirements: Discuss the light requirements of seedlings and ensure they receive adequate sunlight or artificial grow lights for healthy growth.

- Thinning and Transplanting: Guide children in thinning out overcrowded seedlings and transplanting them into larger containers as they grow. Emphasize the importance of giving plants space to grow and develop strong root systems.

5. Monitoring Growth and Progress:

- Observation: Encourage children to observe their planted seeds and propagated cuttings regularly, noting any changes in growth, leaf development, or root formation.

- Recording Observations: Have children record their observations in their garden journals, including dates of planting, germination, and transplanting, as well as growth milestones and any challenges encountered.

- Celebrating Success: Celebrate the success of planted seeds and propagated cuttings as they grow and develop. Encourage children to take pride in their accomplishments and share their progress with others.

6. Harvesting and Enjoying Fruits of Labor:

- Harvesting Produce: As plants mature and produce fruits or vegetables, involve children in harvesting and enjoying the fresh, homegrown produce from the greenhouse.

- Tasting and Cooking: Encourage children to taste and cook with the fruits and vegetables they have grown, fostering a connection to healthy eating habits and the satisfaction of growing their own food.

Through planting and propagating activities, children develop important gardening skills, including seed sowing, seedling care, and propagation techniques. They also gain a deeper understanding of plant life cycles, botany, and the rewards of nurturing living things. These hands-on experiences instill a sense of responsibility, curiosity, and appreciation for the natural world, laying the foundation for a lifelong love of greenhouse gardening and environmental stewardship.

Starting seeds indoors

Starting seeds indoors is an excellent way for kids to kick start their greenhouse gardening journey, allowing them to observe the magical process of seed germination and seedling growth up close. Here's a detailed guide on how children can start seeds indoors for their greenhouse garden:

1. Seeds:
   - Seed Variety: Introduce children to a variety of seeds suitable for indoor starting. Choose seeds of vegetables, herbs, flowers, and fruits that are well-suited to greenhouse growing and easy for children to handle.
   - Seed Source: Provide children with high-quality seeds from reputable suppliers to ensure successful germination and healthy seedlings.

2. Gathering Materials:

- Seed Starting Containers: Gather seed trays, peat pots, or recycled containers for starting seeds indoors. Use containers with drainage holes to prevent waterlogging.

- Seed Starting Mix: Use a sterile, well-draining seed starting mix or potting soil for planting seeds. Avoid using garden soil, which might contain diseases, pests or weed seeds.

3. Preparing Containers:

   - Fill Containers: Have children fill seed trays or pots with seed starting mix, leaving a small gap at the top for watering.

   - Labeling: Label each container with the name of the plant species and the date of planting to keep track of seed varieties and germination times.

4. Planting Seeds:

   - Sowing Depth: Teach children the appropriate sowing depth for each type of seed, as indicated on seed packets. Generally, larger seeds are planted deeper, while small seeds are sown shallowly,

   - Spacing: Instruct children to space seeds evenly within each container to prevent overcrowding and competition for nutrients.

   - Covering Seeds: After sowing seeds, lightly cover them with a thin layer of seed starting mix to provide insulation and moisture retention.

5. Caring for Seedlings:

- Watering: Demonstrate the proper watering technique to children, ensuring that the seed starting mix is evenly moist but not waterlogged. Use a gentle misting spray or watering can to avoid disturbing seeds.

- Temperature and Light: Place seed trays in a warm, brightly lit location indoors, such as near a south-facing window or under grow lights. Monitor temperature and light levels to ensure optimal conditions for seed germination and seedling growth.

- Thinning Seedlings: As seedlings emerge and grow, teach children to thin out overcrowded seedlings to allow for adequate space and airflow. Remove weaker or smaller seedlings, leaving the strongest ones to grow.

6. Transplanting Seedlings:

- Harden Off: Before transplanting seedlings into the greenhouse, help children harden off seedlings by gradually acclimating them to outdoor conditions. Start by placing seedlings outdoors for short periods in a sheltered location, gradually increasing exposure to sunlight and wind over several days.

- Transplanting: Once seedlings are hardened off, guide children in transplanting them into larger containers or directly into garden beds in the greenhouse. Teach them proper planting techniques, such as digging holes and gently firming soil around seedlings' roots.

7. Monitoring and Recording Progress:

- Observation: Encourage children to observe their planted seeds and emerging seedlings regularly, noting any changes in growth, leaf development, or root formation.

- Recording Progress: Have children record their observations in their garden journals, including dates of planting, germination, and transplanting, as well as growth milestones and any challenges encountered.

- Celebrating Success: Celebrate the success of seeds starting indoors as seedlings grow and develop. Encourage children to take pride in their accomplishments and share their progress with others.

Starting seeds indoors provides children with a tangible and rewarding introduction to greenhouse gardening, fostering curiosity, responsibility, and a sense of connection to the natural world. Through hands-on experiences with seed germination and seedling care, children develop important gardening skills and gain a deeper appreciation for the magic of plant life.

Transplanting seedlings into the greenhouse

Transplanting seedlings into the greenhouse is an exciting milestone in the journey of greenhouse gardening for kids. It marks the transition from nurturing seeds indoors to establishing young plants in their permanent growing environment. Here's a comprehensive guide on how children can transplant seedlings into the greenhouse:

1. Preparing Seedlings:

- Timing: Ensure that seedlings are ready for transplanting based on their size, growth stage, and weather conditions. Usually, seedlings should have developed several true leaves and sturdy stems before transplanting.

- Hardening Off: If seedlings have been started indoors, help children harden off seedlings by gradually exposing them to outdoor conditions, such as sunlight, wind, and temperature fluctuations, for a week before transplanting.

2. Preparing the Greenhouse:

-Cleaning: Before transplanting, ensure the greenhouse space is clean and free of debris, weeds, and pests. Make sure to remove any spent plants or materials from previous growing seasons.

- Soil Preparation: If planting directly in the ground, prepare the soil by loosening it with a garden fork or tiller and incorporating organic matter such as compost or aged manure to improve soil structure and fertility.

3. Transplanting Process:

- Watering Seedlings: Water seedlings thoroughly before transplanting to help reduce transplant shock and facilitate root establishment.

- Digging Holes: Demonstrate to children how to dig planting holes in the greenhouse soil or planting beds, spacing them according to the recommended spacing for each type of plant.

- Planting Depth: Instruct children to plant seedlings at the same depth as they were growing in their containers, ensuring that the soil level matches the level of the seedling's root ball.

4. Transplanting Techniques:
    - Handling Seedlings: Teach children to handle seedlings gently by their leaves or root ball, avoiding damage to the stems or delicate roots.
    - Planting Seedlings: Guide children in carefully placing seedlings into the prepared planting holes and backfilling with soil, gently firming the soil around the base of each seedling to provide support.

5. Watering and Mulching:
    - Watering After Transplanting: After transplanting, water seedlings thoroughly to settle the soil around their roots and provide hydration. Use a gentle watering can or hose

with a soft spray attachment to avoid dislodging seedlings.

- Mulching: Optionally, apply a layer of organic mulch, such as straw, shredded leaves, or wood chips, around seedlings to help retain soil moisture, suppress weeds, and regulate soil temperature.

6. Monitoring and Care:

- Observation: Encourage children to monitor transplanted seedlings regularly for signs of stress, such as wilting or yellowing leaves. Prompt them to observe changes in growth and development as plants acclimate to their new environment.

- Watering Schedule: Establish a regular watering schedule for transplanted seedlings, ensuring they receive adequate moisture without becoming waterlogged. Teach children to water deeply and consistently, especially during hot or dry periods.

- Pest and Disease Management: Teach children to monitor transplanted seedlings for signs of pests or diseases and take appropriate action to address any issues. Encourage natural pest control methods and organic gardening practices.

7. Celebrating Success:

- Acknowledging Achievements: Celebrate the successful transplantation of seedlings into the greenhouse with children, acknowledging their efforts and accomplishments. Encourage them to take pride in their role as caretakers of the greenhouse garden.

Transplanting seedlings into the greenhouse is a rewarding and educational experience for children, providing them with valuable lessons in plant care, responsibility, and stewardship of the environment. Through hands-on participation in the transplanting process, children develop important gardening skills and deepen their connection to nature.

Propagating plants from cuttings and divisions

Propagating plants from cuttings and divisions is a fascinating aspect of greenhouse gardening for kids, allowing them to expand their garden by creating new plants from existing ones. It's a hands-on activity that teaches children about plant reproduction and propagation techniques. Here's a comprehensive guide on how children can propagate plants from cuttings and divisions in the greenhouse:

1. Understanding Plant Propagation:
   - Introduction: Explain to kids that plant propagation is the process whereby new plants are created from existing ones, either through seeds, cuttings, or divisions.
   - Types of Propagation: Discuss two common methods of propagation: propagating from cuttings, where a portion of the plant is removed and rooted to grow into a new plant, and propagating from divisions, where a

mature plant is divided into smaller sections, each capable of growing into a new plant.

2. Selecting Plants for Propagation:
   - Suitable Candidates: Help children identify plants that are suitable for propagation from

cuttings or divisions. Choose plants that are healthy, disease-free, and have vigorous growth.

   - Easy-to-Propagate Plants: Introduce children to plant species that are easy to propagate, such as herbs (e.g., mint, basil), succulents (e.g., jade plant, aloe vera), and perennial flowers (e.g., lavender, sedum).

3. Preparing for Propagation:
   - Tools and Materials: Gather the necessary tools and materials for propagating plants, including sharp pruning shears, clean pots or containers, potting soil or rooting medium, and rooting hormone (optional).
   - Preparation: Ensure that pots or containers are clean and have drainage holes to prevent waterlogging. Fill containers with potting soil or rooting medium and moisten the medium before propagation.

4. Propagating from Cuttings:

- Selection of Cuttings: Show children how to select healthy stems for cuttings, choosing young, non-flowering stems with several nodes (where leaves are attached).

- Cutting Technique: Demonstrate the proper cutting technique to children, making clean cuts just below a node with sharp pruning shears. Make sure to Remove any flowers or buds from the cuttings.

- Rooting Medium: Explain different rooting mediums that can be used for propagating cuttings, such as water, perlite, or vermiculite. Help children prepare containers with the chosen medium.

- Rooting Process: Guide children in inserting cuttings into the rooting medium and maintaining optimal conditions for rooting, including consistent moisture and indirect light.

- Transplanting: Once cuttings have developed roots, teach children how to carefully transplant them into individual pots filled with potting soil. Emphasize gentle handling to avoid damaging the delicate roots.

5. Propagating from Divisions:

   - Selection of Parent Plant: Identify mature plants that can be divided into smaller sections for propagation. Plants with multiple stems or clumps of growth are good candidates for division.

   - Division Technique: Demonstrate to children how to carefully dig up the parent plant and divide it into smaller sections using sharp pruning shears or a garden knife. Make sure each section have its own set of roots and shoots.

   - Planting Divisions: Help children plant each division into its own pot or container filled with potting soil, ensuring that the roots are spread out and covered with soil. Water the divisions thoroughly after planting in order to settle the soil around the roots.

6. Care and Maintenance:

- Watering: Instruct children to water newly propagated plants gently but thoroughly to ensure that the rooting medium or potting soil is evenly moist. Please avoid overwatering, which can lead to root rot.

- Light and Temperature: Place propagated plants in a warm, brightly lit location with indirect sunlight. Monitor light and temperature levels to provide optimal growing conditions for root development and plant growth.

- Protection from Pests and Disease: Teach children to monitor propagated plants for signs of pests or diseases and take appropriate action to address any issues. Encourage them to practice good hygiene and sanitation to prevent the spread of pests and diseases.

7. Celebrating Success:

- Observing Growth: Encourage children to observe and track the growth of propagated plants over time, noting any changes in foliage, roots, or overall plant health.

- Sharing Achievements: Celebrate the success of propagating plants from cuttings and divisions with children, acknowledging their efforts and accomplishments. Encourage them to share their propagated plants with friends, family, or fellow gardeners.

By propagating plants from cuttings and divisions, children gain valuable hands-on experience in plant reproduction and propagation techniques. They learn about the life cycle of plants, develop important gardening skills, and gain a sense of pride and accomplishment in creating new life from existing plants. These hands-on activities foster curiosity, creativity, and a deeper connection to the natural world, making greenhouse gardening a rewarding and educational experience for kids.

Chapter 7: Caring for Plants in the Greenhouse

Caring for plants in the greenhouse is essential to ensure their health, vitality, and productivity. For kids engaging in greenhouse gardening, learning how to care for plants is not only practical but also educational and rewarding. Here's a comprehensive guide on how children can care for plants in the greenhouse

Watering and fertilizing tips for kids

Absolutely, teaching kids how to water and fertilize plants in the greenhouse is crucial for their success as young gardeners. Here are some age-appropriate tips and techniques:

Watering Tips for Kids:

1. Consistency is Key:

- Explain to kids that plants need regular watering, but not too much or too little. Consistent moisture helps plants grow strong and healthy.

- Encourage them to establish a watering schedule and stick to it, checking the soil moisture before watering each time.

2. The Soak and Wait Method:

- Show kids how to water plants thoroughly until water starts to drain out from the bottom of the pots or containers.

- Explain that they should then wait for a few minutes to allow the soil to absorb the water before adding more. This prevents overwatering and ensures the roots get the hydration they need.

3. Watering at the Base:

- Teach kids to water plants at the base rather than on the leaves. Watering the leaves can lead to disease and fungal issues.

- Demonstrate how to aim the watering can or hose close to the soil surface to deliver water directly to the root zone.

4. Observation Skills:

- motivate kids to pay close attention to their plants after watering. If any signs of wilting or drooping is noticed, it might indicate that the plant needs more water.

Fertilizing Tips for Kids:

1. Start with the Basics:
 - Explain to kids that plants need nutrients to grow, just like people need food to stay healthy.
 - Introduce them to basic fertilizers such as compost or diluted liquid fertilizer, emphasizing that these provide essential nutrients for plant growth.

2. Less is More:
 - Teach kids that too much fertilizer can harm plants, so it's essential to use it sparingly and follow the instructions on the package.
 - Show them how to measure out the correct amount of fertilizer and mix it with water before applying it to their plants.

3. Timing is Everything:
 - Explain that fertilizing should be done at specific times during the growing season, such as when plants are actively growing and producing new leaves or flowers.

- Help kids create a fertilizing schedule based on the needs of their plants and the recommendations on the fertilizer packaging.

4. Safety First:
- Emphasize the importance of safety when handling fertilizers. Remind kids to wash their hands after fertilizing and to keep fertilizers out of reach of pets and younger siblings.

By teaching kids these watering and fertilizing tips, you're not only helping them care for their greenhouse plants but also instilling valuable gardening skills and fostering a deeper appreciation for nature.

Pest and disease management

Managing pests and diseases in the greenhouse is an essential aspect of greenhouse gardening for kids. By learning how to identify and address common issues, children can protect their plants and foster healthy growth. Here's a guide on pest and disease management tailored for kids:

1. Prevention is Key:
   - Teach kids the importance of preventing pest and disease problems by maintaining a clean and healthy greenhouse environment.
   - Encourage them to practice good hygiene, such as removing fallen leaves, debris, and weeds, to eliminate hiding places for pests and reduce the risk of disease.

2. Regular Monitoring:
   - Show kids how to inspect their plants regularly for signs of pests, such as chewed

leaves, holes, or sticky residue, and symptoms of diseases, such as spots, wilting, or yellowing.

- Explain that early detection allows for prompt action, preventing pests and diseases from spreading and causing more significant damage.

3. Integrated Pest Management (IPM):

- Introduce kids to the concept of Integrated Pest Management (IPM), which emphasizes using a combination of cultural, mechanical, biological, and chemical control methods to manage pests while minimizing harm to the environment.

- Help them identify non-chemical control methods, such as hand-picking pests, using insect traps, and creating physical barriers to protect plants.

4. Natural Predators:

- Teach kids about beneficial insects and other natural predators that can help control pest populations in the greenhouse, such as ladybugs, lacewings, and predatory mites.

- Encourage them to create habitats for beneficial insects by planting flowering plants and providing shelter, such as bug hotels or nesting boxes.

5. Organic Remedies:

- Introduce kids to organic pest and disease control methods that are safe for plants, people, and the environment.

- Show them how to make homemade remedies, such as insecticidal soap (made from liquid soap and water) or neem oil spray (made from neem oil and water), to deter pests and treat minor infestations.

6. Safe Handling of Chemicals:

- If chemical control methods are necessary, teach kids how to use pesticides safely and responsibly.

- Emphasize the importance of reading and following label instructions, wearing protective clothing and gear, and applying pesticides only as directed.

7. Disease Prevention:
   - Explain to kids that diseases can spread through contaminated soil, water, tools, and plant debris.
   - Encourage them to practice good sanitation by disinfecting tools, pots, and surfaces regularly and avoiding overwatering, which can promote fungal diseases.

8. Learning from Experience:
   - Encourage kids to keep a garden journal to record observations, pest and disease problems encountered, and the methods used to address them.
   - Use these experiences as opportunities for learning and problem-solving, empowering kids to become more knowledgeable and proactive greenhouse gardeners.

By teaching kids about pest and disease management in the greenhouse, you're not only helping them protect their plants but also fostering a sense of responsibility, curiosity, and environmental stewardship. These valuable skills will serve them well as they continue to explore the wonders of greenhouse gardening.

Pruning, staking, and training plants for healthy growth

Some of the most important practices in greenhouse gardening for kids include Pruning, staking, and training plants. These techniques help ensure plants grow strong, healthy, and productive. Here's a guide on how kids can effectively prune, stake, and train plants for optimal growth:

Pruning:
1. Purpose of Pruning:
   - Explain to kids that pruning involves removing certain parts of a plant, such as dead or diseased branches, to encourage healthier growth, improve airflow, and maintain the plant's shape.
   - Emphasize that pruning also stimulates new growth and encourages the plant to focus its energy on producing flowers or fruit.

2. Tools for Pruning:

- Introduce kids to basic pruning tools like pruning shears or scissors. Teach them how to handle these tools safely, emphasizing the importance of wearing gloves to protect their hands.

3. Pruning Techniques:
- Show kids how to identify the parts of the plant that need pruning, such as dead or damaged branches, and how to make clean cuts just above a leaf node or bud.
- Demonstrate different pruning techniques, such as thinning out crowded branches or shaping the plant to encourage a more compact growth habit.

Staking:
1. Purpose of Staking:
- Explain to kids that staking helps provide support to tall or heavy plants, preventing them from falling over or bending under their own weight.

- Emphasize that staking also helps improve air circulation around the plant and keeps fruits or flowers off the ground, reducing the risk of rot or disease.

2. Materials for Staking:
   - Show kids various staking materials like bamboo sticks, wooden dowels, or metal rods. Let them choose the appropriate size and strength of stakes for the plants they're growing.

3. Staking Techniques:
   - Demonstrate how to insert stakes into the soil near the base of the plant without damaging the roots. Show kids how to use soft ties or twine to secure the plant to the stake, making sure not to tie too tightly to allow for growth.

Training:
1. Purpose of Training:

- Explain to kids that training plants involves guiding their growth in a specific direction or shape to maximize space and aesthetics.

- Show them how training can help encourage plants to produce more flowers or fruit and make it easier to harvest.

2. Training Methods:

- Demonstrate different training methods, such as gently bending or tying branches, depending on the plant's growth habit. Encourage kids to be creative and experiment with different shapes and forms.

3. Regular Maintenance:

- Teach kids that pruning, staking, and training are ongoing tasks that require regular attention throughout the growing season.

- Encourage them to check their plants regularly for signs of new growth or changes in shape, and adjust their pruning, staking, or training as needed.

By teaching kids how to effectively prune, stake, and train plants, you're not only helping them become better gardeners but also instilling valuable skills and a deeper appreciation for the natural world. These practices empower kids to take care of their plants and create a thriving greenhouse garden they can be proud of.

Chapter 8: Harvesting and Enjoying the Fruits of Your Labor

In greenhouse gardening, harvesting refers to the process of gathering ripe fruits, vegetables, herbs, or flowers that have reached maturity and are ready for consumption or use. Harvesting is a crucial stage in the growth cycle of plants and marks the culmination of the gardening process. It involves carefully selecting and picking the produce at the peak of ripeness to ensure optimal flavor, quality, and nutritional value.

Knowing when to harvest

Knowing when to harvest is a crucial skill in greenhouse gardening for kids. It involves observing and understanding the signs that indicate fruits, vegetables, herbs, or flowers are ready for picking. Here's how kids can learn to recognize the right time to harvest:

1. Color and Size: Teach kids to look for visual cues such as vibrant colors and proper size. Fruits and vegetables often change color as they ripen, becoming brighter or more intense. For example, tomatoes turn from green to red, while peppers change from green to yellow, orange, or red. Similarly, fruits and vegetables should reach their mature size before harvesting.

2. Texture and Feel: Encourage kids to gently touch and feel the produce to assess its texture. Ripe fruits and vegetables are often firm but yield slightly to gentle pressure. They should feel plump and heavy for their size. Teach kids to avoid harvesting produce that feels too hard or soft, as it may be underripe or overripe.

3. Smell and Aroma: Show kids how to use their sense of smell to detect the aroma of ripe produce. Many fruits and herbs develop a fragrant scent as they ripen, signaling that they are ready for harvest. For example, ripe

strawberries have a sweet, fruity aroma, while basil emits a strong, aromatic scent when ready for picking.

4. Taste Testing: Encourage kids to taste-test a small sample of the produce to assess its flavor and sweetness. While not all fruits and vegetables are suitable for tasting raw, many can be sampled to determine their ripeness. For example, cherry tomatoes, strawberries,

and snap peas are safe and delicious options for taste testing.

5. Observation and Patience: Teach kids the importance of patience and observation in determining when to harvest. Encourage them to visit the greenhouse regularly to check on the progress of their plants and look for signs of ripeness. Remind them that it's better to wait a little longer for produce to ripen fully than to harvest it too soon.

By learning to recognize the signs of ripeness, kids can develop a deeper understanding of plant growth and the natural world. Knowing when to harvest allows them to enjoy the fruits of their labor at the peak of freshness and flavor, making greenhouse gardening a rewarding and satisfying experience for young gardeners.

Harvesting techniques for kids

Teaching kids proper harvesting techniques in greenhouse gardening is essential for ensuring that they gather fruits, vegetables, herbs, and flowers effectively while minimizing damage to the plants. Here's a guide on how to introduce kids to various harvesting techniques:

1. Hand Picking:
    - For many crops, especially berries, tomatoes, and peppers, hand picking is the most common harvesting technique.
    - Teach kids to gently grasp the fruit or vegetable with their fingers and twist or pull it from the plant's stem.
    - Emphasize the importance of being gentle to avoid bruising or damaging the produce.

2. Using Scissors or Pruners:
    - Introduce kids to small, child-safe scissors or pruners for harvesting crops with tougher

stems or thicker foliage, such as herbs or flowers.

- Show them how to use the tools safely, making clean cuts just above a leaf node or stem junction.

- Teach them to hold the stem steady with one hand while carefully cutting with the other to avoid accidentally cutting nearby plant parts.

3. Snapping or Breaking:

- Some crops, like snap peas or beans, can be harvested by snapping or breaking them off the plant.

- Demonstrate to kids how to grasp the pod or bean firmly with one hand and use the other hand to snap it cleanly from the stem.

4. Twisting:

- Certain crops, such as cucumbers or zucchinis, can be harvested by gently twisting them from the plant.

- Show kids how to grasp the fruit near the base and twist it gently until it separates from the stem.

5. Cutting with a Knife:

- For crops with thick stems or roots, such as melons or root vegetables, a knife may be necessary for harvesting.

- Teach kids to use a sharp knife safely and responsibly, making clean cuts without damaging the plant or surrounding foliage.

6. Checking for Ripeness:

- Before harvesting, instruct kids to check for ripeness by examining the color, size, and texture of the produce.

- Encourage them to look for visual cues, such as vibrant colors, firm textures, and mature sizes, to determine if the crop is ready to be harvested.

7. Handling Fragile Produce:

- For delicate crops like berries or cherry tomatoes, emphasize the importance of handling them with care to prevent bruising or squashing.

- Teach kids to cradle the fruit gently in their hand while harvesting to minimize damage to the delicate skin.

8. Harvesting Leafy Greens:

- For leafy greens such as lettuce or spinach, demonstrate how to harvest by cutting individual leaves or clusters of leaves from the outermost part of the plant.

- Encourage kids to harvest only what they need, allowing the inner leaves to continue growing for future harvests.

9. Celebrating the Harvest:

- After harvesting, celebrate the bounty of fresh produce or flowers with kids by admiring their harvest and discussing how they plan to use or share it.

- Encourage them to take pride in their efforts and to appreciate the rewards of greenhouse gardening.

By teaching kids these harvesting techniques in greenhouse gardening, you're helping them develop valuable skills and knowledge while fostering a deeper connection to nature and the food they eat.

Conclusion

As we come to the end of our journey through "Greenhouse Gardening for Kids," I hope you've discovered the magic and wonder that the greenhouse holds. From the first sprout peeking through the soil to the bounty of fruits, vegetables, and flowers ready for harvest, greenhouse gardening has offered us a glimpse into the beauty and abundance of the natural world.

But our journey doesn't end here—it's just the beginning. As you continue to tend to your greenhouse garden, remember the lessons you've learned along the way. Embrace the joy of discovery, the satisfaction of hard work, and the awe-inspiring resilience of nature. Let each day in the greenhouse be a new adventure, filled with growth, learning, and connection.

And as you watch your garden flourish and bloom, remember that you are not just a gardener—you are a steward of the Earth, entrusted with the care of its precious resources. By nurturing your greenhouse garden with love and respect, you are making a difference in the world, one seed at a time.

So, whether you're harvesting your first ripe tomato or planting a row of fragrant herbs, know that you are part of something bigger than yourself. You are part of a community of gardeners, young and old, who share a passion for growing, learning, and living in harmony with nature.

Thank you for joining me on this journey through "Greenhouse Gardening for Kids." May your greenhouse garden continue to inspire and delight you for years to come. Happy gardening!

Bonus: Recipes and crafts using greenhouse-grown produce and flowers

Here are 21 recipes and crafts using greenhouse-grown produce and flowers:

Recipes:

1. Caprese Salad Skewers:
   - Thread greenhouse-grown cherry tomatoes, fresh mozzarella balls, and basil leaves onto skewers. Drizzle with balsamic glaze and serve as a refreshing appetizer.

2. Greenhouse Herb Pesto:
   - Blend greenhouse-grown basil, parsley, and garlic with olive oil, pine nuts, and Parmesan cheese to make a flavorful pesto. Toss with pasta or use as a spread for sandwiches and wraps.

3. Stuffed Bell Peppers:

- Fill greenhouse-grown bell peppers with a mixture of quinoa, black beans, corn, and diced tomatoes. Top with cheese and bake til the peppers are tender.

4. Fresh Tomato Salsa:
   - Dice greenhouse-grown tomatoes, onions, and jalapenos. Mix with chopped cilantro, lime juice, salt, and pepper for a delicious salsa to serve with tortilla chips or tacos.

5. Cucumber Avocado Salad:
   - Slice greenhouse-grown cucumbers and avocado. Toss with cherry tomatoes, red onion, and a lemon vinaigrette for a refreshing salad.

6. Herb-Roasted Chicken:
   - Rub greenhouse-grown herbs like rosemary, thyme, and sage onto chicken pieces. Roast in the oven till it's golden brown and aromatic.

7. Grilled Veggie Skewers:

- Thread greenhouse-grown vegetables such as zucchini, bell peppers, and mushrooms onto skewers. Grill until tender and serve as a healthy side dish.

8. Strawberry Spinach Salad:

- Toss greenhouse-grown spinach with sliced strawberries, feta cheese, and toasted almonds.

Drizzle with a balsamic vinaigrette for a savory and salad sweet.

9. Herb-Roasted Potatoes:

- Toss greenhouse-grown potatoes with olive oil, garlic, and chopped herbs like thyme and rosemary. Roast until crispy and golden brown.

10. Tomato Basil Bruschetta:

- Combine diced greenhouse-grown tomatoes with chopped basil, garlic, and olive oil. Serve on toasted baguette slices for a classic Italian appetizer.

11. Herb-Crusted Salmon:

- Coat salmon fillets with a mixture of greenhouse-grown herbs, breadcrumbs, and olive oil. Bake until the fish is cooked through and the crust is crispy.

12. Zucchini Noodles with Pesto:

- Spiralize greenhouse-grown zucchini into noodles. Toss with homemade pesto and cherry tomatoes for a light and flavorful pasta alternative.

CRAFTS:

13. Pressed Flower Art:

- Press greenhouse-grown flowers between the pages of a heavy book. Once dried, arrange them on cardstock or canvas to create beautiful floral artwork.

14. Herb-Infused Candles:

- Fill small jars with soy wax and greenhouse-grown herbs like lavender, mint, or rosemary. Once cooled, trim the wick and enjoy the soothing aroma when lit.

15. Flower Crown:
    - Create a flower crown using greenhouse-grown blooms like daisies, roses, and baby's breath. Secure the flowers onto a wire or ribbon base for a whimsical accessory.

16. Potpourri Sachets:

- Fill small muslin bags with dried greenhouse-grown flowers and herbs. Tie with a ribbon and place in drawers or closets for a natural air freshener.

17. Herb-Stamped Tea Towels:
   - Dip greenhouse-grown herbs in fabric paint and stamp onto plain tea towels to create unique botanical designs.

18. Floral Bath Bombs:
   - Mix dried greenhouse-grown flowers, Epsom salt, baking soda, and essential oils to make homemade bath bombs. Mold into shape and allow it dry before use.

19. Scented Herb Wreath:
   - Create a wreath using dried greenhouse-grown herbs like lavender, sage, and rosemary. Hang in the kitchen for a fragrant and decorative touch.

20. Floral Potpourri Ornaments:

- Fill clear glass ornaments with a mixture of dried greenhouse-grown flowers and herbs. Use as room decor or Hang on a Christmas tree.

21. Herb-Infused Vinegar:
 - Fill a glass bottle with vinegar and add greenhouse-grown herbs like thyme, basil, or dill. Let infuse for a few weeks before using as a flavorful salad dressing or marinade.

These recipes and crafts showcase the versatility and beauty of greenhouse-grown produce and flowers, allowing you to enjoy their bounty in both culinary and creative endeavors.

Made in United States
Troutdale, OR
05/16/2024